IT DOESN'T HAPPEN BY ACCIDENT

The 6 Keys to Leading with Intention

ETHAN MILLER

WHAT OTHERS ARE SAYING ABOUT
IT DOESN'T HAPPEN BY ACCIDENT

"I read *It Doesn't Happen by Accident* yesterday -- I was a better teacher today! Thank you Mr. Miller for your brilliant book. Thank you Mr. Tan for your life-changing advice."

Rob Gilbert, Ph.D.
Professor of Applied Sport Psychology
Founder of Success Hotline

"Ethan Miller's new book ought to come with a warning label:

CAUTION: EDUCATORS, DO NOT READ THIS BOOK UNLESS YOU WANT TO DEEPEN YOUR IMPACT AND TRANSFORM YOUR CAREER.

Because that's what WILL happen if you read it."

John Brubaker
Best-Selling Author of Stadium Status:
Taking Your Business To The BIG TIME

"If you are serious about making a difference and becoming a person of influence, this book is a must read!"

"Ethan's message of Leading with Intention resonates with adults and students alike, and is one of the most impressive books I have read in my years in education."

"Ethan has put his passion for personal development into one of the best books I have ever read. Everyone needs a coach to continue to grow and this is a read that all leaders will benefit from."

"You can change your attitude or change your environment. This book illustrates the steps anyone can take to change their attitude, when maybe changing the environment isn't an easy thing to do. If you are just getting started on the path to self-mastery, or maybe you need a quick refresher, I highly recommend this quick read! You won't regret it!"

Leslie Huntington, M.Ed.
National Champion Head Softball Coach
University of Wisconsin-Eau Claire

Ethan Miller
Compete Publishing

It Doesn't Happen by Accident
The 6 Keys to Leading with Intention

© 2017 by Ethan Miller

Printed in the United States of America

Edited by: Mary Lou Reynolds
Cover by: Miljan Jovanovic

ISBN: 978-1547153084

IT DOESN'T HAPPEN BY ACCIDENT

The 6 Keys to Leading with Intention

INTRODUCTION

Brian Morris is in his second year of teaching Science at Chapman High School. Chapman High School is a moderate-sized school with an enrollment of 350 students in grades 9-12. Along with Brian's responsibilities in the classroom, he also is the head of the Student Council.

Brian's teaching career did not get off to the start he had anticipated. Coming out of college, he took the first job that was offered to him as a way to get his foot in the door. His plan is to spend two years at Chapman and then move on to a bigger school, much like the one he had attended.

Brian knows he is at a crossroads in his teaching career. He is on his last year of his Initial License, where he is not completely certified by the state Board of Education. Brian must show he is competent in each of the state standards and benchmarks before he obtains his Standard License. This has to happen if he wants any shot at moving on to another school.

He is having a difficult time connecting with his students and their standardized test scores have dropped since he arrived. Brian's principal, Mrs. Cruise, has been patient with him and is doing her best to be a mentor without being overbearing. However, the list of complaints she has received from the students and parents due to his teaching procedures and general attitude has put her in a position where time is running out.

Mrs. Cruise has tried to push Brian to other teachers for help and he has tried to make connections with all of the teachers. However, each staff member is too busy working within his or her own room so he naturally keeps to the teachers in his wing of the building. The layout of the building is confusing due to a shoddy addition project a few years back – teachers on one end of the building are now completely disconnected from the other end and have to take a figure eight loop through two different doors to get to the opposite end.

With the challenge of the building layout, he hasn't taken the time to travel to the other side, especially since there is a parking lot outside his door and the teacher's lounge is right across the hall.

Brian began the year looking to start off on the right foot and to model what his teachers did when he was in high school. However, his motivation quickly disappeared and by the time the first semester ended, he was no better off than he was at the end of his first year; he could see the writing on the wall. Brian was considering leaving education altogether to take a job at a laboratory in his hometown that paid better and would still allow him to use his Science degree.

It wasn't until one fateful day in March that he encountered the man who would change his life forever...

CHAPTER 1

Field Trip

It had already been "one of those days" and it was only 9:00 am. Luckily, it was a Wednesday so the weekend was coming, and I could not wait to get out of here and head back home to hang out with my buddies.

The first period of the day was horrendous. The students had, once again, failed to get their assignment done so I had to redo the entire lesson on the fly, which ended up being a catastrophe. Seriously, I never turned my homework in late and wouldn't have imagined not even doing it. I sure let those kids have it.

It seems that this generation of young people wants everything spoon-fed to them, and if the solution doesn't come to them at warp speed, they give up and merely will not do it. This feels like an unwinnable battle.

After a quick refill of my coffee from the staff lounge across the hall, the guidance counselor, Mr. Jackson, was in my classroom waiting for me. This was my prep period and I needed to get planning on my next three sections of freshmen before they arrived. The only motivation of the day was that we had an early dismissal for an afternoon of Professional Development and didn't have to be in front of students.

"Hey, Mr. Morris," said Mr. Jackson, who stood tall next to my whiteboard looking at the lesson I had just attempted to teach the previous class.

"Hi, Mr. Jackson. What can I do for you?" I responded with an inquisitive tone. Mr. Jackson only comes down to visit when Mrs. Cruise is busy and needs a message relayed – I swear it's because she wants him to spy on me.

"Well, you're going to have a little bit of a break coming up here. It seems that Mrs. Palmer forgot to tell the staff that the freshmen would be leaving at 9:15 am for a field trip to see *Les Miserables* at the university, so you will have the rest of your morning open until teacher in-service begins after lunch," Mr. Jackson said.

This is music to my ears. What an incredible break! I get the next three hours off to do as I please within my classroom. There is a stack of labs that I need to grade that have been staring at me for over a week, but I just have not felt like doing them.

"Thanks for the heads-up, Mr. Jackson. Looks like I've got some time to work here in my room," I said with a definite excitement.

"Well, actually that won't be the case," Mr. Jackson said hesitantly.

"Okay. What's going on?" I said with raised eyebrows and open eyes in a defiant way, since he was apparently going to take my free time away as quickly as it was granted.

Mr. Jackson said, "Mrs. Cruise wants you to head down to the gymnasium and map out the layout for the upcoming Senior Citizens dinner that the Student Council is responsible for, and she needs it by lunchtime so she can coordinate with the cook staff and the custodial staff on what needs to be done to prepare for next week."

"Sounds good," I replied and Mr. Jackson went on his way. You could feel the tension in the room being immediately released.

CHAPTER 2

Wasting Time

As I left my classroom, I swung by the teacher's lounge to refill my coffee cup one more time before heading down to the gym. While in the room, I ran into Mr. Wright, a veteran Science teacher of 25 years whose classroom is next to mine.

Mr. Wright has seen it all in his career and gets it. I can have honest conversations with him and he knows how different things are today. I will say, though, that our "honest conversations" are more like complaining sessions, but they can still be productive.

When I first met him two years ago, I thought he was really negative and a downer, but after I got to know him, he really makes a lot of sense. The experience he has in teaching has been a big help to me.

"What's going on, Brian?" Mr. Wright asked.

"Not much. Heading down to the gym to do the layout for the Senior Citizens dinner next week. Mrs. Cruise wants me to do that now since the freshmen are gone on a field trip," I replied.

"Typical," he sneered. "Don't you love it how, when you actually get some free time in the day to work, the administration makes you do some meaningless task? I swear people don't ever think around here. This afternoon of in-service is going to be another pointless activity thrown our way where something from 20 years ago gets re-packaged with a fancy name and delivered as a new idea. What a waste of time. Good thing I've only got one more year here until retirement."

I nodded in agreement because what I've learned in my time with him is that there is no point in arguing – he will just keep spinning you into the web of his beliefs, so you might as well go along with it. I sure do hate in-services, though, but it's good with Mr. Wright because we do our own thing anyway and have some nice free time.

After telling him goodbye, I made the trek down to the opposite end of the building, surviving the maze of confusion. There's a good reason why I don't come down here, for it's a pain in the butt and takes forever. I swear you need a passport to get here!

I could feel my frustration building because of the conversation with Mr. Wright and because getting down here was taking away precious time from my classroom. However, any time away from the students was fine by me; I needed a break.

The gym happened to be open and the Physical Education classes were using the fitness center. As I drew up the layout, I found a stray basketball in the corner and took a few shots. I really enjoyed being a basketball player in high school. It was just too bad that I tore my ACL before senior year and missed that season. We could have done something special.

Before I knew it, 20 minutes had passed by and I still needed to draw out this layout for the dinner.

I was halfway to completing the diagram when I received a phone call from my older brother Troy.

Troy has it all going for him. He is a successful football coach at a Division 2 school and his wife Carrie is one of the top triathletes in the country. Carrie's grandmother had recently passed away from a long battle with cancer. He informed me that they would be flying in on a red-eye to the airport one hour away from me on Thursday night. I told him I would pick them up and offered them a place to stay. My two-bedroom apartment isn't much but it will do for their time here. He was very gracious and accepted.

I always feel better when I talk to my brother. I am envious of his positivity and outlook on life.

As I picked up the basketball for a couple last shots, my mind began to wander. "How did I get to this place I am at today, where I dread each day? Once the weekend comes, I am happy again but then quickly switch back to this person on Monday. This can't be all there is, right?" Deep down I know I am not where I need to be as a person but have no idea what I need to do to get there.

It had been 90 minutes since Mr. Jackson came down to my room and I was still not finished with the diagram. The motivation to do anything had completely left. I sloppily put together a diagram and walked out of the gym.

As I left the gym, I heard a sound that didn't seem to belong in a school setting. It was the sound of blaring music, clapping, and laughter.

I followed the sound down around the corner to a part of the building I had never seen and saw something that rocked me to my core.

CHAPTER 3

Mr. Tan

Following the sounds, I peeked around the corner of the hallway and witnessed a scene that I had never imagined would be inside of a school.

I felt like I was slapped in the face with energy and enthusiasm. The music was blaring and the students were on their feet clapping to the beat of the Dimitri Vegas & Like Mike song "The Hum." I was in awe of the connection each student had with the others and was shocked to see some of my afternoon science students, who display zero emotion or personality, jumping around and giving high-fives to everybody in sight.

At the front of the room was the ringleader. He was a tall, athletic man who looked to be in his early 40s and in phenomenal shape. He had a level of presence about him that I had not seen before in an educator. We have roughly 40 staff members and I have seen him before at meetings and Professional Development, but our paths hardly ever crossed for I was always following around Mr. Wright.

I stood back in the hallway. Once the bell rang, the class silenced, the music stopped, and the students began to work.

My mind was racing. "Who in the world is this guy? How did he get them to all be quiet and start working without yelling? Why does it feel like I'm seeing him for the first time?" I needed answers.

I looked at the entrance to his room and there it was on a laminated piece of paper:

Mr. Harrison Tan
Social Science Instructor

Lucky for me there was a section of the hallway that jutted out so I could hang back behind it without being seen, yet I could hear everything.

After a 3-minute period of students quietly working, Mr. Tan said to the class, "Welcome to the most important class period of your life. What we do here in the next 42 minutes matters. Let us all treat it as such."

I was immediately inspired, yet also suspicious. There must be something more to this guy than meets the eye. He spoke to his students with sincerity but was also very sharp and to the point. Either these students believed in him or feared him. Whatever way you look at it, his classroom operated in a way that got my attention.

Time was ticking, but I knew that I wanted to stay for a little bit longer. Mr. Tan commanded the students to get out their Journals in preparation for the day's mindset piece. He opened up a book called *The Daily Dominator* and read a selection from today's date.

Today's selection was about finding a coach, similar to that which an Olympic athlete or UFC fighter has. The message was about finding the right person to lead you, for too much negativity will drag you down or too much sunshine will give you a false sense of reality. There needs to be balance. As I stood there listening, my mind went to Mr. Wright and I thought, "He has naturally led me since I got here. Is he the right coach for me?"

While I was staring into the classroom and thinking, one of my junior students, Jason, caught me. We locked eyes and he made an interesting gesture. He nodded his head in the direction of Mr. Tan, almost to say through ESP, "This is the guy you need as your coach."

Like a nervous teenager who got caught staring at the pretty girl in class, I immediately looked away and started walking back to my classroom. Two hours had passed since I initially left to go lay out the gym for the Senior Citizens meal so I briskly walked back through the maze to my classroom to do some work before in-service. When I arrived at my classroom, I could not focus and the image of Jason nodding towards Mr. Tan was tattooed on my mind; I was unable to shake it.

CHAPTER 4

In-Service

I managed to grade a few lab reports and got back to what needs to happen inside of my classroom. Mr. Wright came by before lunch, like he does every day, and we walked to the cafeteria, which is in the middle of the building. After grabbing our lunch trays, we headed to the teacher's lounge to eat.

The 30 minutes in the lounge is a nice time to talk with other teachers and to hear the war stories of the morning. Early on, I did a lot of listening but I feel comfortable now bringing up things that happened in the morning or struggles that I am having. Every so often the conversation turns negative, which isn't so bad because we all need a place to blow off some steam.

I returned to my classroom to close up a few items before the teacher in-service meeting started at 1:00 pm.

We gathered in the library as a staff to go over the day's activities. We were to have a presenter taking us through new ways to assess student learning within our teaching areas. As the meeting opened up, I quickly found Mr. Tan.

In-services are an interesting exercise; most teachers look at them as a burden and I certainly did not care for them. After my encounter with Mr. Tan's class this morning, I was eager to see how he responded to this environment.

I sat with my usual collection of teachers, including Mr. Wright. As the presenter began, Mr. Tan sharpened his focus and was an absolute machine. I observed the people around my table and they were doing things like checking e-mail, looking at their NCAA tournament bracket, or searching for items on Amazon. Mr. Tan? His computer was closed, notebook out, and he was engaged the same way his students were in his class.

I asked Mr. Wright, "What is it with Mr. Tan? What's his story?"

"Oh, him?" exclaimed Mr. Wright. "That's Harrison Tan. He's been teaching Social Sciences here for 35 years."

"35 years?!" I replied extremely surprised. "The guy looks like he's in his early 40s!"

Mr. Wright continued, "He's actually older than I am. I believe he just turned 58. He has been eligible to retire for the past 5 years and he's an idiot for staying in education when he doesn't need to. He's a good guy, but we don't see eye-to-eye on many things so we have a working relationship and that's it. I tell you what, I cannot wait to be done teaching and will not work one more day than I need to before I can retire."

The rest of the in-service I took on as a game to see if I could match the level of focus that Mr. Tan had. Wow – was it hard! I am 24 years old and this 58-year-old was absolutely crushing me and he had no signs of slowing down.

I realized it was a game I was going to lose, so went into my Google Drive folder to correct some vocabulary assignments until we were able to leave at 4:00 pm.

It had been an interesting day, to say the least, and one that opened my eyes. Mr. Tan had been there for all this time, yet I was just discovering him and learning about him from afar.

On the way home back to my apartment, which is roughly two miles from Chapman High School, I stopped at a grocery store to grab a frozen pizza and a 6-pack for the NBA game that was on that night between the Spurs and Warriors. I should have brought the labs home to grade and help save me some time, but whenever I bring something home, it never gets done. It is pointless to do so.

CHAPTER 5

The Airport

My Thursday at Chapman High School was average at best. The students still were emotionless and I did not seem to connect with them. It is becoming increasingly hard to deliver instruction when the message that I am sending does not appear to be received by my students. Classroom management problems are rising and more students are testing me and my authority, if you can even call it that.

My brother Troy and his wife Carrie were flying in at midnight so I was going to just stay up until it was time for me to make the hour drive to pick them up. I reluctantly stayed after school until 6:00 pm grading labs and, I will admit, it felt really good to have that off my plate. I drove home and cleaned the apartment and prepared the spare bedroom for Troy and Carrie before heading to get them at 11:00 pm.

Their flight was right on time and it was so good to see them both again.

"Great seeing you, bro!" exclaimed Troy as he hugged me and lifted me off the ground. "Wish it were under different circumstances but always a good feeling to be around family."

"I agree." I turned to hug Carrie and she gave me a kiss on the cheek. "I'm so sorry for your loss, Carrie."

"Thank you. I appreciate that but it is for the best. She lived a great life and now it's time for us to celebrate the life that she lived and the legacy she left," Carrie said.

We loaded up my Jeep and made the hour drive back to my apartment. We had great conversation about anything and everything; I always feel so much better when I am around them.

Their week will be pretty busy with the planning of the funeral and the different family that will be coming in. They asked if they could borrow my Jeep for the time they are here since they'll need to do a lot of running around. I obliged since I don't live too far away from school and my Jeep would just stay in the parking lot anyway. The plan was for Troy to drop me off each morning and then I would walk back each night. This worked out well for they are morning workout people and would be up anyway.

It was 2:00 am before we finally settled down. I am not going to be teaching very hard tomorrow after this late night excursion. I should just call in sick.

CHAPTER 6

Walking Home

It's a good thing I have people staying with me in this apartment for there was no way I would have woken up on time. We didn't get to bed until 2:00 am and both these lunatics were up at 5:00 am and ran five miles before waking me up.

"I swear you are adopted, Troy," I said to my older brother as I raced to the coffee pot to get the caffeine into my bloodstream.

A quick shower and I was off to school. Troy dropped me off at the front of the building and, as older brothers do, he had to make a smart comment: "Have a good day, sweetheart! Be nice to your friends and say please and thank you!"

In my current state of sleep deprivation, I was not in the mood. I nodded and went on my way to my classroom doing my best not to appear like a zombie from *The Walking Dead*.

The day came and went with more of the same as before. I'm really starting to stress out about getting my Initial License converted to a Standard License. I have all of the answers and theory to how science works but cannot get my students to learn it at the rate they need to. The job at the lab back home is looking like more of an option as each day passes.

The reality is this: It is March, there are two months of school left, and I am no better off now than I was a year ago. My students consistently underachieve and no matter how much I beg and plead, it is not working. Throw in the increased number of referrals and parent complaints; I know I'm riding front seat on The Struggle Bus. Ugh.

There was nothing left to do once the final bell rang so I cleaned up my workspace to appear to the custodians who clean my room, and anybody else who may look in here, that I am organized and somewhat competent.

Not having a vehicle to drive home was going to be different for the next week but I could manage. It was only a two-mile walk and my mornings were taken care of. I could use the exercise anyway and it would give me a chance to listen to some music during the 30-minute walk to my apartment.

I started off through the parking lot and onto the sidewalk by Highway 20, the main road that cuts through town. As music played through my earbuds while I waited for traffic by the stoplight, I heard the honking of a horn that startled me in a big way. I removed my earbuds and looked to my left to see Mr. Tan in his black pickup. He rolled down the passenger side window as I stared at him and said, "Hey, Brian. You need a lift?"

CHAPTER 7

Happy Hour

I couldn't believe what was going on right now. How crazy is this?!

My immediate response to Mr. Tan's inquiry was, "Nah, I'm okay. I don't live that far away. I don't want to inconvenience you."

"Well, that's good you don't want to inconvenience me. I appreciate that," responded Mr. Tan. "However, I offered you a ride and it's about to rain, so you might as well hop on in."

He was definitely right about the rain and I was happy to escape the dark clouds as they rolled in. I opened the door to the truck and climbed aboard.

"Glad to have you in here, Brian, and happy we finally get a chance to connect. It's about time we were formally introduced since we've been working in the same building for two years now. My name is Harrison Tan." As he extended his hand to shake mine, I felt an immense sense of calm over take my body as if I had known this man my entire life.

"Pleasure to meet you, Mr. Tan," I replied. "My name is Brian Morris. I really appreciate the ride."

"Absolutely! Fired up to do so," he exclaimed with an energy that was uncommon for a Friday after school when most people were looking to escape and win the race with the kids out of the building to their cars in the parking lot.

"What do you have going on tonight, Brian?" Mr. Tan asked me as we stopped and waited for the light to turn green at the main intersection outside of Chapman High School.

"Not much," I replied. "My brother and sister-in-law are in town for the week for a funeral so I will probably just head back to my apartment and watch some TV tonight. I'm heading to my hometown to see some of my buddies on Saturday and Sunday so will figure out a way to get back since my brother is using my Jeep while they're here."

"Sounds like you got it all figured out," Mr. Tan answered back as he turned on his wipers now that the rain was starting to fall. I was really happy he stopped, for I would have been on my way to getting poured on.

"Well, before I take you back to your date with the TV," Mr. Tan joked, "how about we grab a bite? You hungry?"

I most definitely could eat – I had skipped breakfast to squeeze out a few more precious moments of sleep after the late-night airport run, and the cookies that the cook staff put in the lounge before lunch had seemed just fine at the time.

"That sounds good to me!" I responded, trying not to seem too anxious at the invitation to join him. Believe it or not, the only people I had been out with socially since arriving a year and a half ago were Mr. Wright and the other veteran teachers. It was usually a good time, but it always seemed to turn into a gripe-fest about Chapman High School and its students. I could use some new scenery.

We stopped at a place called *Lavoie's,* which I had been by a few times yet never managed to pull the trigger to go in – always a difficult thing to go someplace by yourself.

"This is my favorite spot for Happy Hour on Fridays," Mr. Tan said excitedly as he looked around the place, almost searching for something. I quickly realized what that was.

"Hey, you," came from the voice of a beautiful brunette over by the bar section of the restaurant. I guessed that this was his wife and that she was much younger than he. However, if my judgment of age was anything like that of Mr. Tan, I'm sure they were probably the same age.

"You're late, Mr. 168!" she jabbed in his direction. Must be a nickname or something.

"Sorry, babe. Had to make a pit stop to pick up a new friend to join us for our Friday tradition," he explained as her smile beamed at him. "Becky, I would like for you to meet Brian Morris, who is a Science teacher at Chapman and in his second year. Brian, this is my wife of 30 years, Becky."

"Pleasure to meet you, Becky," I replied while I extended my hand to shake hers. "No thanks, Brian. If Harrison says you're a friend, we can do much better than that," Becky stated as she extended her arms wide for a hug. I had never been around two people so positive and uplifting and yet had only been around them for less than 10 minutes.

The waiter led us to the Tans' "usual spot" at *Lavoie's* and we immediately dove into conversation. We shared everything, from my background growing up that led me to Chapman, to how they met 31 years ago at this very place on a Friday and vowed to continue to meet when schedules permitted.

The Tans lived very busy lives. Becky was a successful education consultant who also had a background in Science so we hit it off immediately, especially our passion for Physical Science.

They have two girls who are grown up and have families of their own and see them as much as possible, but they are steadfast in still living their own lives and "executing their mission," as they put it.

We talked about my beginnings as a teacher and the challenges that I faced within my classroom. They both listened so intently that I felt as if the chair in *Lavoie's* was a couch in a psychiatrist's office.

We discussed my transportation dilemma with my brother and sister-in-law in town and when I explained that, they casually looked at each other through the corner of their eyes, smiled, and placed their attention back on me.

As the night drew to a close, I was beyond grateful for the opportunity to meet them and to connect on such a deeper level. Hopefully this would happen more often. I offered to pay for them in thanks, which they denied; and when I attempted to take care of my portion of the bill, they explained, "When we were your age, we had an older couple take us out and did for us what we are doing here for you. Our only request is that you do the same someday when you are in our position."

I graciously accepted and only hoped that that day would come.

Mr. Tan and I said goodbye to Becky. I knew better than to give her a handshake and went in for a hug. "It was a pleasure to finally meet you, Brian," she said, and I thought to myself, "*Finally?*"

CHAPTER 8

The 6 Keys to Leading with Intention

Mr. Tan and Becky said goodbye and that they would see each other later, after I was dropped off and after Becky made a quick stop to fill up her Acadia on the way home.

As I directed Mr. Tan on the short trip to my apartment, I expressed my gratitude for the night. "The pleasure was ours, Brian," he responded earnestly.

He pulled his black pickup into my apartment parking lot and as I was saying goodbye, he said to me, "Tell you what. I drive by your apartment each day on my way to Chapman High School, so it seems silly for your brother to drive you. I'll come back each morning this coming week and take you. How's that sound?"

I was thrilled with the offer and accepted.

As I shook his hand in thanks, I exited the truck and started to walk toward my apartment entrance.

As he put his truck into drive, he rolled down his passenger side window and yelled, "Have a great weekend, Brian. Meet you out here at 6:00 Monday morning. Bring some comfortable shoes too."

That was the straw that broke the camel's back. I waved my arms at him and ran towards his truck. He hit the brakes and looked at me as I asked in desperation, "Why me?"

"What do you mean?" he answered back.

"It seems that today was not fate or happenstance but like I was a part of a plan. Not that I'm complaining, but what gives?"

I realized as soon as I asked that I probably came off extremely rude, but at that point in time I needed answers.

"Well, Brian, I have watched you from a distance in your time here and know that you can use some help. I see a lot of myself in you when I first started teaching 35 years ago. I got into education to change the lives of those students who walked inside of my classroom – to make a difference. What I realized quickly was that I needed to change myself before I could change the lives of others. Luckily for me I had a mentor who helped me become the man I am today, and I want to help you become the person you were destined to become. Do you understand where I'm coming from?"

His comments hit me like a punch to the gut. This is exactly why I was in the position I am today at Chapman. I came into teaching with the greatest of intentions but had lost my way. I needed help.

With eyes wide open and a lump in my throat, all I could muster was, "I completely understand."

Mr. Tan continued, building momentum with every word. "Starting on Monday I am going to teach you *The 6 Keys to Leading with Intention* that I learned from my mentor, Mr. Smid. This has helped me to live life intentionally and to impact the lives of those whom I serve at the highest level. I cannot wait to embark on this journey with you, if you're willing."

"Absolutely!" I exclaimed with a smile on my face, eagerly anticipating what was to come. I had not been this excited for the days ahead in quite some time.

"Right on, Brian! Enjoy your weekend and I will see you right here at 6:00 am on Monday. Oh, and you better have a comfortable pair of shoes," said Mr. Tan and he drove away.

I was jacked up, but quickly came back to Earth and thought to myself, "What the heck are we going to do at 6:00 am on a Monday?"

CHAPTER 9

Key #1 – Make Today Count

My weekend back home with my buddies was a blast as always but my thoughts were preoccupied with what was to come with my time with Mr. Tan.

It was amazing how quickly he was able to cut to the core of me and what it was that I needed. No wonder I was struggling with my students – for if this guy can read me that easily after only a few hours, my students had to have a firm grasp of me after over a year.

My friends Bryce and Josh drove me back since Troy and Carrie were using my Jeep for the week. After a quick stop at Buffalo Wild Wings for some Opening Day baseball, we made the two-hour drive back to my apartment.

Normally on Monday mornings I don't wake up until 6:00, so to be ready to go by 6:00 am, especially on a Monday, required extra motivation. Troy and Carrie were up for a morning workout at 5:00 so I reluctantly woke up when they did to prepare for my time with Mr. Tan.

Like clockwork, as if I expected him to somehow forget, Mr. Tan was right on time and I was greeted by the blaring sounds of the AC/DC song *Thunderstruck* pumping from his truck speakers.

"Morning, sunshine! Ready to dominate the day?" he proclaimed in question form, but it was more of a command than a question.

"You got it," doing my best to match his energy, for I was only on my second cup of coffee and needed a bit more before I could fully function.

"Gosh, I love Mondays," Mr. Tan hollered out as he turned down the music ever so slightly. "This is the opportunity to start fresh, brand new, and to get out on the attack." I wish I shared his enthusiasm.

Mr. Tan continued, "Last Friday we had a great time together and I could tell that you were motivated. Well, today is the day to prove it. The true test of motivation is doing what you said you were going to do, long after those feelings have left.

"I want to share with you *Key #1 – Make Today Count*," Mr. Tan said and I immediately was intrigued. "What do you suppose that means, Brian?"

My mind does not like to function this early so I was scraping through the fog to get to a somewhat sane answer. "I suppose it has something to do with the importance of today?" I responded.

"Exactly right, Brian. Do you know what holiday today is?" he asked me. Man, this guy loves questions.

"I have no idea. National Ice Cream Day?" I replied.

"Not a chance, my man. It is the Holiday of Today. This day, today, is the most important day of your life. When your eyes cracked open this morning, you were blessed with another 24 hours and an opportunity to impact this world and those whose path you cross. You would be doing yourself, and everybody else, a disservice by treating it just as another day," Mr. Tan said with building volume and intensity.

We arrived in no time at Chapman High School to an empty parking lot, which happened to be the one closest to my classroom. We got out of his pickup and walked towards to my room with our bags and shoes in tow.

When we arrived at my classroom, Mr. Tan told me to put my shoes on and that it was time to get on the move.

"What are we doing now?" I asked in confusion.

"It's time to walk the halls," he replied. "I walk the halls from 6:00-7:00 each morning. The purpose this serves is twofold: For starters, it gets me moving first thing in the morning, and a little morning sweat is always the best remedy to shake off whatever sleep is left over. And finally, it gets my mind right to focus on those students who will occupy these hallways in a short couple hours. It is my responsibility to be at my best today to help them be at their best."

The way this guy talks is awesome and I was taking mental notes as we moved about the building, engaging in conversation about the building's history and greeting the custodians as they prepared for another day.

"Let me ask you this, Brian," Mr. Tan commented as we were in a nice groove to our walk. "If you were to have woken up with $86,400 in your bank account with the stipulations that you could not save it or invest it and any money left over would be taken away from you at the end of the day, what would you do?"

"I would spend every single penny," I quickly responded as to mirror the tempo of his speech.

"Exactly!" he cried out. "However, we do not have that luxury in the form of money but we do have it in the form of time. We have 86,400 seconds each day to make a difference and cannot afford to leave anything left over. Too often people today do exactly the opposite of what I'm talking about here with Key #1. People count the days instead of making the days count."

"Brilliant!" I thought to myself as he talked about how today is never promised to us; it never has been and never will be again.

Mr. Tan continued, "If you ask every staff member and student in this building if they want to have a great life, the resounding response would be 'Yes.' However, in order to have a great life, we need to be focused on having great moments. In order for us to have great moments, we need to give the best gift of all to those around us – our presence."

This was hitting home with me on a new level. As we had been walking for 45 minutes now, I felt a level of focus that hadn't been with me since high school basketball practice. I was more prepared mentally to teach than ever before.

Mr. Tan concluded, "So here is your action plan for today, for knowledge without action means nothing. Within your classroom, I want you to W.I.N. and focus entirely on What's Important Now. Be present with your students and what you're delivering to them. Remember, all we have is today, so you better make sure that it's your best work. Give everything you have to your students and watch what happens in return."

As we separated at 7:00 am, I had already sweated through my undershirt, so I adapted and removed it in the bathroom and collected myself before preparing for my day.

In my morning preparations, I found a new focus on today and what I needed to do to maximize the 86,400 seconds given to me. This was so new and such a different way of going about my business, but I really enjoyed how I felt with this newfound motivation.

As each class entered the room, I greeted them all with smiles and even had some light music playing in the background. This was met with some interesting looks from the students, almost as if to say, "What's up with this guy?"

I greeted them all with the statement, "Good morning, class. It's an honor to be with you today, which happens to be the most important day of your life. Why, you might ask? Because this is the only day that you're living and it is up to us to not just count the days, but to make the days count. Let's all make today count."

CHAPTER 10

Key #2 – Function over Feeling

Wow! Yesterday was one of the best teaching days that I've ever experienced. I actually felt a fun buzz in the classroom and students seemed to respond in an improved way. However, I did notice that it completely zapped me and I was extremely tired this morning. I knew that Mr. Tan would be coming to get me at 6:00 am like yesterday, but I was moving considerably slower – I was not used to the tempo of teaching that I took part in yesterday.

As I went about my morning in preparation for the day, I told myself, "Today is the only day that matters; let's get after it." However, this did not change my mood.

Mr. Tan's black pickup pulled up and I jetted out the door to get in. I was very appreciative of the ride and knew that I better play by his rules, so to speak.

"Hey there, Brian. How are you this morning?" Mr. Tan asked and I could tell that he was probing me for more than the usual response.

"I'm okay. Yesterday was awesome and I thank you for *Key #1 – Make Today Count*. However, the pace of the day yesterday completely gassed me. I'm tired and my legs are a little sore from our hour walk yesterday morning," I said.

"So what? Since when does how you feel have anything to do with it?" he replied.

"Huh?" I questioned back, fully knowing he would somehow respond with some incredible statement that would bring it all full circle.

"Glad you asked, Brian. This brings us to *Key #2 – Function over Feelings*," said Mr. Tan. "The most dangerous sentence in the world is *I don't feel like it*. When you said that you were sore and tired, that was you playing into your feelings instead of your level of function."

As we entered the building the same way that we did the day before, to go to my classroom and begin our walk, I started to think deeply about what he had said already this morning. I swear this man can cover more material in a two-mile drive than anybody else known to man.

We started on our walk and he continued to preach. "Brian, we need to listen to ourselves less and talk to ourselves more. When we talk to ourselves, we focus intently on what we need to do, instead of what we feel like doing. Nobody ever got anywhere in this world by doing what they felt like doing. It all came down to action."

As we walked by a student's locker that was left open from the previous day, there was a picture of Chicago Cubs pitcher Jake Arrieta inside the door. Mr. Tan quickly jumped on that image and said, "There is a Cy Young Award winner and World Series Champion who understands the importance of action. Underneath the bill of his cap he has the letters A.C.E., which stands for Acting Cures Everything. For us to be successful today we need to act differently than how we feel."

As my mind raced, I posed a question back to him for greater explanation. "Well, if we act differently than how we feel, won't that make us fake?"

"Great question, Brian. It comes down to a simple question: 'Are you a professional or are you an amateur?' You see, it is about doing what is necessary in your role as an educator to deliver quality instruction to those students who sit at the desks," Mr. Tan said.

As we continued to talk, I noticed that we were once again 45 minutes into the walk, and the feeling of tiredness and soreness had gone away because I was simply in a state of doing.
"That makes sense. I think my biggest pitfall as a teacher thus far has been falling victim to my feelings instead of how I need to

function. What can I do to make this better?" I inquired.

"Well, our morning walk is almost over so it comes down to application," he said. "In order to change how you function, just remember your ABCs and to get BIG. You must Act Big, Breathe Big and Commit Big."

He continued, "Your physiology, or body language, has a direct relation to how you function psychologically, or what levels of confidence and positivity you experience.

"Another way to look at it is to Always Behave Confidently. Know that confidence is a choice and make the decision to stand tall, get your shoulders back, and go out on the attack."

As we parted ways after another walk, I reflected upon how I was carrying myself in the classroom. No wonder my Period 1 class can smell my fear and anger, based upon my body language and how I've functioned. I've never been a self-proclaimed "morning person" but did feel more prepared in the two days I had walked before school.

I've also noticed things with my veteran co-worker Mr. Wright. His body language is atrocious and he is carrying himself based upon how he feels, not by how he needs to function to lead his students.

How could I not have seen all of this before? It was as if my formal education in college had not served me as well as the life education I was receiving from Mr. Tan.

CHAPTER 11

Key #3 – Principles over Preference

Wednesday. It is halfway through the week. Hump Day.

I took a deep breath as my alarm clock sounded, and I sat up in my bed and stared off towards the floor in my bedroom for a good five minutes, running through every possible excuse as to why I wasn't going to actively participate in this day.

The two days I have experienced thus far have been transformational but it seems impossible each day to repeat the actions of the day before. I could feel the emotion overtaking me and justifying to myself what I was feeling.

However, at that exact point in time, I remembered Mr. Tan telling me, "You must act differently than how you feel and then you will begin to feel the way you need to be acting." Gosh, I wish it were that easy!

I eventually made it vertical and out to the main living space of my apartment. As I greeted Troy and Carrie after their workout, I kept doing what Mr. Tan told me to do – just act and everything else will fall into place.

I rushed to gather my things and just as I put my last shoe on, Mr. Tan pulled up as he had done in the previous days. He is the most consistent person I have ever met.

As I approached his pickup, I wondered what song of choice he would have for me today. When I opened the door, I heard the voice of a strange South American man named Andy who was talking about the body.

"What is this?" I questioned Mr. Tan as he brought his focus back towards me and hit pause on his iPhone.

"This is an app called *Headspace*," he explained. "It is a way for me to live according to my One Word for the final quarter of the school year."

"What do you mean, One Word?" I asked. It is phenomenal how I can walk to his pickup and have a good idea about what is about to transpire yet be in complete awe once it occurs.

"Each quarter of the school year, I outline a One Word for me to focus on that will help direct me to how I need to function and to live a life that is reflective of my Core Principles," he said with a glimmer in his eye. "Which leads me to *Key #3 – Principles over Preference*."

I loved the direction he was going. My dad taught me that the best predictor of future behavior is past behavior, so when Mr. Tan spoke, I knew something legit was about to come out of his mouth.

As we arrived at the school just after 6:00 am like the previous mornings, this day's talk resonated with me in a different way.

"So, Mr. Tan, I have to ask you – what do you mean by One Word to focus on and Core Principles? Okay, I guess it is a question with two responses, but I need more," I asked him. No longer was I feeling tired, but invigorated.

"Haha," he laughed at my query. "I get it, Brian. Time to giddy-up!" Upon this response he cracked his knuckles and tilted his neck as to get ready to drop some psychological genius on me.

As we laced up our shoes in my classroom, he dove right in.

"Let me first begin by talking about Core Principles. These are the characteristics that you value in your life that will help drive your behavior. Living a life based upon principles will allow you to eliminate the gray areas and to hone in on those actions that will get you closer to your desired goals and outcome."

I nodded in his direction and my mind was once again racing.

"So how is living according to your Core Principles different than what we talked about in Key #2, Function over Feelings?" I asked him, and yet surprised myself at the level of question-asking I have reached in only a few days. There is complete comfort and trust here and I am not afraid to appear needy, for I obviously needed all of this.

"They are one and the same, my friend," he casually responded. "Function and principle live in the same place. The only difference is that function works better when there is a set of principles to support."

"So what are your Core Principles?" I asked and already was considering a number of them in my own mind. Perseverance. Discipline. Commitment. Energy. Attitude.

"The Core Principles I live by are through the acronym S.E.E.K.," he explained to me and immediately placed a vision in my mind. "This stands for Selfless, Energy, Excellence, Knowledge. Every decision that I make in my life is in relation to these Core Principles and, like I mentioned before, they drive my behavior to function according to these principles."

The principles he laid out did not shock me in any way, shape, or form for he truly lives them.

"So how about your One Word focus? How is that different?" I prodded.

"The One Word focus can be a reflection of your Core Principles or an area of your life that needs more attention. My One Word focus for the final quarter of school is Empower. I want to empower each of the students who walk inside of my classroom to know they have the ability to create a life that they deserve. They have zero control of what happens to them in life but complete control of how they respond to it. The life they want is for the taking; all they have to do is go get it and realize they can have it," Mr. Tan said with increasing conviction. I would have done anything to have a teacher like him when I was in school.

"So where do I begin?" I asked him as I gazed down at my watch and realized that we were nearing the end of our hour-long walk.

"Do you know what my favorite time is, Brian?" he asked with a huge smile on his face.

"No clue, my man," I responded.

"Application time!" he exclaimed and continued. "Start by identifying one Core Principle in your life and how you can live it daily. After you have done so, look deeper to where you need more attention and establish a One Word focus for the remainder of the school year that will be a reflection of your Core Principle. Remember, Brian, a boy acts out of preference but a man acts out of principle."

As we parted ways and I was thinking about all that he had said this morning, the last comment he made hit me the deepest. Too long have I gone into the school and made decisions based upon what was comfortable instead of what was necessary.

The silence of the school was calming, as it allowed me to close my eyes and think about how I wanted to live. After a few short moments, it all became clear.

My Core Principle was Purpose. I have a mission to execute each day to impact the lives of those whom I serve at a deeper level. My One Word focus would be Action. I want to be a person of action who puts aside what is convenient in favor of what is necessary.

This exercise was like a gigantic energy shot to my soul. I made it my goal to teach that day as a reflection of my Core Principle of Purpose, for these students needed me in their journey. It was like a switch was flipped and I had blinders on like those of a Clydesdale horse.

Everything was starting to come full circle. I felt different, but more importantly, I was acting differently. Others around me started to take notice, including Mr. Wright, who made a comment after I declined to eat lunch in the lounge in favor of preparing for upcoming lessons in the afternoon: "Careful there, young buck. What you're doing is impossible to sustain over the course of your career."

"Watch me," I replied with some big body language and intent like I had never felt before.

CHAPTER 12

Key #4 –
You Become
Your Habits

The week was drawing to a close, but as I had learned just a few short days ago, we are not going to count the days and look too far ahead but rather are going to make the days count.

Waking up was not as difficult as it was earlier in the week and, in fact, I actually looked forward to it.

When my alarm clock sounded at 5:00 am, I popped out of bed and was the first person out to the kitchen for coffee. This was the first time in my entire life that I woke up earlier than my older brother Troy!

When he and Carrie saw me in the kitchen, he exclaimed, "Whoa! Look at this guy getting up early and getting after it!" I sure did feel good about myself and the progress I was making.

Mr. Tan had been well worth the price of admission and had impacted my life more than anybody else ever had before. My classes were responding to my newfound mission and the students actually were enjoying what was taking place within Science. Mrs. Cruise did a walk-through observation yesterday and for once I was not startled and nervous – I was confident and excited for her to witness what was happening. She gave me a huge smile of approval and was shocked to see the level of engagement by not just the students, but by me in delivering quality instruction. I could not be prouder to live according to my principle of Action and One Word focus of Purpose.

Bright-eyed and eager, I arrived at my apartment parking lot earlier than the other mornings. In fact, I was so early that I wondered if Mr. Tan had forgotten me.

Of course, Mr. Tan arrived right on time at 5:55 am with a honking horn and flashing headlights.

"Look out, world! Here comes Brian Morris and he is out on the prowl looking to dominate!" he yelled and immediately set the tone for the day.

"You got it, Mr. Tan! No longer am I going to be a bump on the log of life. I've never been so excited to execute today's mission and ready to learn about Key #4," I blared towards him in anxious anticipation like a baby bird waiting for a worm. I could not get enough.

"Let me ask you something, Brian," he directed my way. "Was it easier or harder for you to wake up on time this morning when compared with Monday?"

"Way easier. It was almost effortless and I cannot believe how good I feel, even though feelings have nothing to do with it," I exclaimed. My comments brought a big smile to his face.

"Well, Key #4 is all about what you are feeling right now – *You Become Your Habits*," he said; and at that time, just like in the days before, we arrived at school and it was time to roam the halls.

As we started off on our walk, we shared stories of bad, yet harmless, habits that we have in our lives that we wish we could kick. I told him that I bite my nails and have ever since I was in elementary school when I had a nail bent back at recess. Since that day I could not stand having a longer nail that could impede my performance. Mr. Tan shared that each night he locks his front door twice, just to be sure he and Becky are secure, even though they live in a very safe neighborhood.

"So when you started biting your nails, Brian, did you think to yourself that you would be still doing it 15 years later?" he asked.

"No way. All I was doing was getting rid of an issue so that I could keep playing. It wasn't until later on that I realized I had a bad habit on my hands," I replied.

"That is the thing about habits that make them so hard to break. If you were to take one single strand of hair and try to break it, could you do it?" he asked.

"Of course. It would be easy," I replied.

Mr. Tan then asked, "How about if I bundled 1,000 hairs together. Would it still be easy to do it?"

"No way. It would be way too thick to break," I answered.

Mr. Tan continued, "That is exactly how habits are formed. They begin as one small strand and, over time, become a tightly wound rope that cannot be broken."

This made all the sense in the world, and then it got me wondering...

"So what habits do you have in your life right now that cannot be broken?" I asked.

"Well, one of them we are doing right now by walking the halls. I have been walking the halls and starting my morning off with movement since I was 30 years old. After Becky and I had kids, I developed some bad eating habits and failed to follow through with the same exercise plan I did in my 20s. This resulted in being 30 pounds overweight and I hated how I felt and how I functioned. I made the decision to start my morning off with exercise at 4:30 am so that I can work on me first, so that I can work on others more effectively," he replied.

"So let me get this straight," I stated in a confused tone. "You work out BEFORE you come walk the hallways?"

"You got it, brother," he said with the swagger of a teenager. "My daily routines and rituals are so engrained into my everyday life that it does not change, no matter the circumstance."

This guy was an absolute machine and something that I could model after. I hated how my body had changed since high school, and part of the reason why I was so sluggish each day was due to my physical state. The mornings we had been walking the halls had improved my general well-being and preparation for the day. This was definitely a practice I could maintain.

"This is what is known as *The Compound Effect*, which happens to be one of my favorite books by Darren Hardy," he said and I quickly took out my iPhone to make a note so I wouldn't forget to check that book out.

"Little by little, everything adds up to something big. Let me ask you this – would you rather have $5 million right now or one penny doubled each day for a month?" he asked. There had to be a catch, but I bit at his quiz.

"Oh, I would take the $5 million right now and twice on Sunday," I replied.

"Well, that one penny doubled every day for a month turns into $10.7 million at the end of the 31st day," he explained.

"You've got to be kidding me?!" I fired back.

"No lie. You see, that is where people fall short in life. The key to long-term success is sticking to your habits and doing a little, a lot. Eventually those small daily decisions become huge difference makers. The way I figure it, walking for one hour each morning before school gets me around 5,000 steps and approximately 2.5 miles. This isn't a huge number, but when I add that up each day of our 190-day contract, that is 475 miles gained for the betterment of my health and well-being," he explained.

"Wow – that is impressive!" I exclaimed at the sheer magnitude of those numbers.
"Become a machine of routine in your life and the results you want will come your way," he explained.

Mr. Tan then said, "As we get ready to start our day, think of this. What can you implement in your everyday personal life and also your classroom that can be bedrock habits where doing a little, a lot, will make massive progress?"

As we broke from our walk, I knew that I needed to start my day off with exercise and a more consistent morning routine so that I was prepared for the day that was to come. Within my classroom, I needed to develop a consistent routine to start class and also to bring closure to class so that there wasn't any mystery to what was taking place. In a world of uncertainty, my students could grab onto the fact that we would be consistent over time in order to reach the goals we wanted to obtain.

Little by little, I used the Compound Effect to my advantage and implemented small routines within my classroom, thinking to myself, "If I want them to get to a certain point, I better map out the plan for them to get there."

Jeepers! Education can be fun when you know what the heck you're doing!

CHAPTER 13

Key #5 – Bring the Energy

Friday has a such a great feel to it. Yes, I know that feelings have nothing to do with it, but there is something about the end of the week that brings so much joy.

Before, I used to think, "Yes, it's over and I don't have to see those kids' faces again for another couple days!" Ever since I've spent time being mentored by Mr. Tan, my thoughts now are, "This is what fulfillment feels like – to know when a job has been done well and it's time to finish it."

I awoke at 4:45 am before my alarm went off and was wide-awake. The decision was made to go outside and do some exercise before Mr. Tan came to pick me up. Troy and Carrie were going off on a long run of 10 miles before the funeral events this morning and I was in no physical shape to do that, so I instead opted for 20 minutes of running with 10 push-ups and 10 sit-ups every 5 minutes of clock time.

At the end of the workout, I was exhausted and immediately regretted doing so. However, as time passed by, I felt a blast of energy take over and this catapulted me to a new level.

As Mr. Tan pulled up, he was all sorts of fired up. I could tell he was a big music guy, but when I opened the door to Macklemore

& Ryan Lewis with "Can't Hold Us" blaring out of his pickup speakers, I knew this would be a unique day.

"What's up, Mooooooorrrriiiisssss?!" Mr. Tan screamed as he was fist pumping to the beat in the song. Seriously, this guy is a teenager. I love it.

"What's up, Taaaaaaaaannnnnnnnnn?!" I echoed back to him.

"Dude, it is Fired-Up Friday and we are going to bring it today. You with me?" he asked, not as a question but as a rally cry.

"You got it, my man! Let's do this," I replied and we were off toward Chapman High School to put Key #4 into action.

As we pulled up into the parking lot and made the same walk to my classroom, we ran into Tom, who was the head custodian at our school.

"Morning, Tom! Great day, isn't it?" Mr. Tan asked.

"Seriously, Harrison, how do you have so much energy every day?" Tom replied with laughter and amazement.

"Well, Tom, we have to make a choice each and every day to get after it, and I'm about to teach Brian here *Key #5 – Bring the Energy*," Mr. Tan professed.

Today's walk had all sorts of pep to it and Mr. Tan was in rare form.

"I just smashed my 5K record this morning, and for being age 58, I'm stoked about it," he said. "I love morning exercise; it's like taking your energy pill each day to fuel you for what is to come."

"No doubt! I got my workout on this morning and feel great and ready to get on the attack," I responded while matching his enthusiasm.

"Brian, you are learning a valuable lesson here about energy. The energy we showcase daily is a choice. We have got to bring the juice," he explained. "For when you are juiceful, you are useful and when you are juiceless, you are..."

"Useless!" I screamed and we high-fived each other and continued on our walk.

"Every day is an opportunity to lift up others around us to new levels. There is no way we can motivate kids to learn with low energy levels. That is why I love music, getting kids out of their seats and onto their feet, and playing quick games. It forces them to bring energy and to infuse it immediately," he explained.

"I'm not going to lie to you. I stumbled upon your class over a week ago when you were having kids jump around and give high-fives, and the energy that came out of that room was intoxicating," I confessed.

"That's awesome! I had no idea you were there. That's the cool thing about energy – it is recyclable. What you give off you are going to get right back in return," he commented while strutting like a proud peacock.

"So what do you do daily to bring the juice?" I asked him.

"For starters, each morning I write three things in my Gratitude Journal. That gets me having a sense of appreciation for all the things I have, and brain research will show you that energy increases when there is a focus on gratitude and appreciation," he said.

"That is a great strategy, Mr. Tan. I'm definitely going to put that into practice. My sister-in-law Carrie just told me this morning before the funeral exercises that we are 'too blessed to be stressed,' and I think that falls into this category," I explained.

"Absolutely, Brian," Mr. Tan replied. "The main strategy I use is being consistently aware of how I am carrying myself and the level of enthusiasm I am displaying to those around me. As leaders, we are the lone street lamp that emits light to our area. I aim to be the lamp that has the most bugs surrounding it and being drawn to it. A brighter light means it will attract more living things. This is why I'm still in the game; I feel that my light can still shine brighter than anybody else's," said Mr. Tan with hands pumping and directing his vision onto me.

"You're an inspiration, sir, and challenge accepted!" I replied.

"And what challenge is this, may I ask?" he inquired.

"The challenge of who can bring the most juice to this school every day. Let's roll!" I proclaimed to him and loved the analogy he used to describe his role as a leader.

As we finished our walk for the week, I waited for more, but he simply kept walking towards his room.

"Hey, Mr. Tan, did you forget something?" I pleaded to him.

"I don't think so. What you got?" he replied.

"Well, the week is over and you've only taught me 5 Keys – you said there were 6. Did you forget to do so?" I asked.

"Absolutely not. I'm saving Key #6 for tomorrow," he replied.

"But tomorrow is Saturday," I responded in confusion.

"Congratulations, Brian. You know your days of the week," he replied sarcastically. "See you at 6:00 tomorrow morning."

CHAPTER 14

Key #6 – 2 + 2 = 5

This was a first for me. I have been teaching for almost two years now and have NEVER gone in on a Saturday, let alone a Saturday morning.

I woke up before my alarm like I had the day before and then something odd happened. I just started moving.

After learning about Key #4, I had established some sound routines such as setting my phone across the room with my workout clothes next to it, as to get out of bed and to exercise. Even though it was a Saturday, I settled in and got after it.

Troy and Carrie were getting their things organized around the apartment. Their flight was tonight, so I would be taking them back up after I invested my morning at Chapman. It was great to have them here, even though our schedules did not allow for much social time.

Mr. Tan pulled up in his black pickup for the last time. It was very bittersweet for I had become a different person over the course of the past week, yet was excited to have my Jeep back and some normalcy to set in to my everyday life.

"Beautiful morning, isn't it?" Mr. Tan asked with as much vigor in his voice as yesterday.

"Gorgeous," I replied. "Can't say I have seen a Saturday morning this early in quite some time, yet I am enjoying the heck out of it."

"Doesn't seem so bad to be up early on a Saturday, does it?" Mr. Tan asked.

"Not one bit. It helps that I've got you here, for that makes it easier when you're with somebody you know," I replied.

"Exactly. And that is *Key #6, 2 + 2 = 5*," he beamed.

We arrived at the school parking lot and walked side by side into the building. It felt like we were two prize fighters walking into the ring ready to do battle. The energy between us was obvious.

"The main point to Key #6 is that of synergy," Mr. Tan said. "You see, we are more than likely to give up on ourselves before we will give up on anybody else. We enjoy the company of others and will go great lengths to satisfy the other person's needs."

"Sort of like being on a team," I replied. "It's easier when we are all working towards a common goal as one cohesive unit instead of a collection of individuals trying to figure it out solo," I explained to him. You could tell that he was proud at how far I'd come over the course of this week, and I wanted to show him that it has not gone without appreciation.

"My cousin has two mules and each of them serves a very important role within the farm." He began his story as we weaved through the first set of curved hallways on our traditional morning walk. "One mule can pull 1,000 pounds and the other mule can pull 1,200 pounds. Math will tell us that when working together they can pull how much, Brian?"

"They can pull 2,200 pounds," I replied as he was trying to catch me not listening.

"Well, why can these two mules pull 2,500 pounds?" he asked.

"Synergy," I replied anxiously like an elementary student who had been waiting all class period to blurt out a response.

"Exactly. High water raises all boats, and we can do so much more when we are working with others towards a common goal. We become like the five people we invest the most time with, and when those five people have common traits and personalities, magical things can happen in terms of growth and development," he explained.

"Like what has happened here this past week," I said to him as he nodded.

Our walk was almost over before we went to our respective classrooms to close up the week that just occurred and to plan for the week ahead. Mr. Tan was always saying how "the separation is in the preparation."

As we finished the walk, I shook his hand and said, "Mr. Tan, I just want to thank you for this week. You have made an incredible difference in my life and I don't know if I will ever be able to repay you for the knowledge, mentorship, and friendship you have given me."

"The pleasure was all mine, Brian," he replied. "However, do not think of this as the end. We have to continue to hold each other accountable to do the things we say we are going to do in executing our mission here at Chapman. This place needs us to be at our best to impact the lives of those who walk through these hallowed halls."

"Well then, until next time!" I stated with enthusiasm and we headed to our rooms.

As I prepared for the week ahead, I was lost in thought about how much more different things would be after the experience with Mr. Tan. I knew clearly that I am meant to be in education, and it was crystal clear how I intend to not only teach Science, but to create masters in the art of living.

I invested four hours at school before heading back to my apartment for lunch and a nap.

The trip to the airport with Troy and Carrie was fun, and we left a little bit earlier so we could stop for dinner on the way over and get caught back up after the whirlwind that was the past week.

They had a lovely time with family in celebrating the life of Carrie's grandmother and enjoyed hearing all the stories. Much of the conversation was directed towards me and the complete turnaround I had made this past week. I shared with them the process of *The 6 Keys to Leading with Intention* that Mr. Tan had explained to me and how the implementation has forever changed the direction of my life.

After dinner I dropped them off at the airport and returned home to some peace and quiet. After tidying up the place, I hit the sack early to catch up on some much-needed rest.

CHAPTER 15

Sunday Morning

I chose to not set my alarm on Saturday night so that I could sleep in a little after the early mornings I had the past week.

It was 8:00 am when I finally made it out of my bedroom and to the kitchen to grab a cup of coffee.

It was a beautiful morning and I was getting the itch to go do something. "Thanks a lot, Mr. Tan," I thought to myself, for apparently my body craved movement early in the day, as it has become a part of my routine.

There was a nearby park with some trails, so I went back to my bedroom to change clothes when I heard the phone ring.

I ran to the living room to grab it and the call was from Mrs. Cruise, the high school principal.

"Hello, Mrs. Cruise! How are you today?" I answered.

"Good morning, Brian. How are you today?" she asked in a monotone voice.

"Outstanding," I replied. "About to head to the trails for some fresh air. What can I do for you?"

There was no response, only silence. I pulled the phone away from my ear to look and see if the call had been dropped. When I saw the timer on the call still moving, I said, "Hello? You still there?"

"Yes, Brian. Unfortunately I have some very bad news. There has been an accident," she replied.

I knew what she was going to say before her words touched my ears and proceeded to hit my heart like a freight train.

"Mr. Tan was involved in an accident this morning and he did not survive. I'm so sorry."

What am I supposed to do now???

WANT TO KNOW WHAT HAPPENS NEXT?

It Doesn't Happen By Accident
Living a Life of Purpose

ABOUT THE AUTHOR

Ethan Miller is currently the Athletic Director at Central Springs High School in Manly, Iowa. Along with his duties as AD, he teaches courses in Character & Leadership, Health, and Physical Education. Ethan also serves as the Mentoring Coordinator for first- and second-year teachers. He is still very involved in coaching, serving as the Head Baseball Coach and Assistant Girls Track & Field Coach.

Ethan garnered all-American honors playing baseball at Northwestern College in Orange City, Iowa, and is a member of the Northwestern College Athletic Hall of Fame. He has a bachelor's degree in Physical Education and a master's degree in Sports Management.

Ethan is co-author of *The Mental Game for Athletic Administration* with Brian Cain, who is the top mental conditioning and peak performance coach in the world. In *It Doesn't Happen By Accident*, Ethan outlines the 6 Keys to Leading with Intention and how to maximize your impact with your school, organization, and life.

He and his wife Becky, who teaches Science in the Central Springs District and is the Head Girls Track & Field Coach, reside in Mason City, Iowa, with their daughters Gretta and Margo.

CONNECT WITH ETHAN
ON SOCIAL MEDIA

 @EthanMiller_20

 emiller2020

Made in the USA
Monee, IL
27 September 2019